A FIRST LOOK AT SNAKES, LIZARDS AND OTHER REPTILES

By Millicent E. Selsam and Joyce Hunt

Illustrated by Harriett Springer

WALKER AND COMPANY
New York

For Greg

First published in the United States of America
in 1975 by the Walker Publishing Company, Inc.

Published simultaneously in Canada by
Fitzhenry & Whiteside, Limited, Toronto.

Trade ISBN: 0-8027-6212-3

Reinf. ISBN: 0-8027-6211-5

Library of Congress Catalog Card Number: 74-26315

Printed in the United States of America.

10 9 8 7 6 5 4 3 2 1

A FIRST LOOK AT SERIES

Each of the nature books for this series is planned to develop the child's powers of observation and give him or her a rudimentary grasp of scientific classification.

What is a reptile?

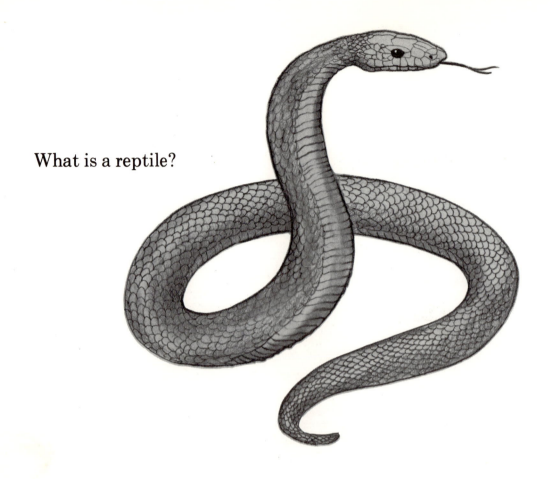

A reptile is an animal with a scaly skin.

Each scale is tough and hard like a fingernail.

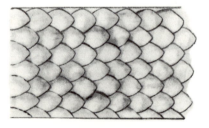

4

This is an animal with a scaly skin.
Is it a reptile?

No, it is a fish.
Fish have fins.
Reptiles do not.

This is another animal with scales
all over its body.
Is it a reptile?

No, it is a mammal.
Mammals have hair or fur.
Reptiles do not.

This is an animal with scales on its legs and feet.
Is it a reptile?

No, it is a bird.
Birds have feathers.
Reptiles do not.

This is still another animal with a scaly skin.
Is it a reptile?

Yes, it is a reptile.
It has scales but—
It doesn't have fins like a fish.
It doesn't have hair or fur like a mammal.
It doesn't have feathers like a bird.

Snakes and lizards are reptiles.
Crocodiles, alligators and turtles
are reptiles, too.

You can easily tell one kind
of reptile from another.

Snakes have no legs.

Lizards look like snakes with legs.

Alligators and crocodiles look like giant lizards.

And, everybody knows a turtle.

LIZARDS

How do we tell one lizard from another?
Sometimes their scales give the clue.

Gila monsters have scales like small beads
that make their skins look bumpy.

Skinks have shiny scales.

Spiny lizards have spiny scales.

Which is which?

13

There are other ways to tell lizards apart.

Find the lizard with a loose and wrinkled skin.

Find the lizard with padded toes.

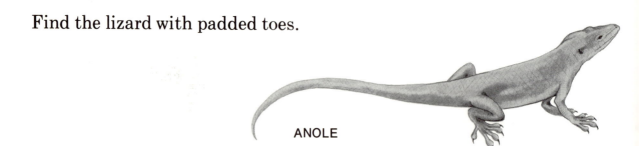

ANOLE

IGUANA

14

Find the lizard with a crest of
spines down its back.

Find the lizard with horns on its head.

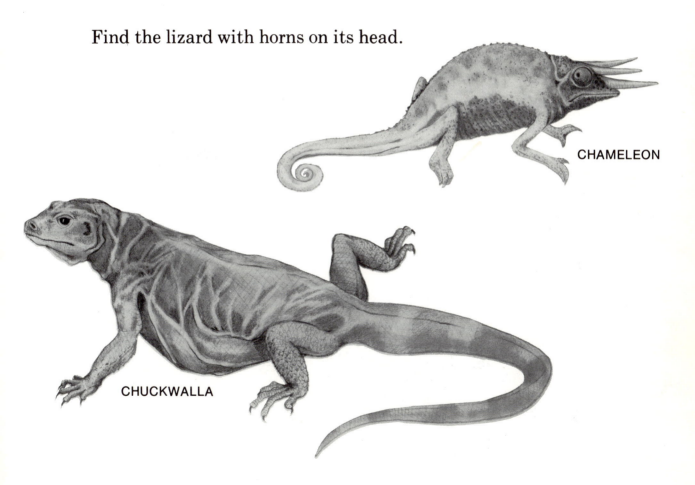

CHAMELEON

CHUCKWALLA

Lizards also have different shapes.

Racerunners have long, skinny bodies
with long, skinny tails.

Horned toad lizards have flat, round bodies
and short tails.

Is this a lizard?

Look at its shape.

It looks like a snake because
it doesn't have legs.

But . . .

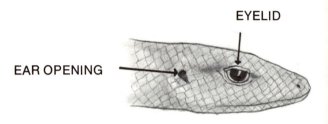

LIZARD

EYELID

EAR OPENING

It is a lizard because—

Lizards have ear openings.
Snakes do not.

Lizards can blink their eyes
because they have eyelids.
Snakes have no eyelids.
Instead, they have a clear,
glassy scale covering their eyes.

SNAKE

GLASSY SCALE

Lizards have several rows of
scales on their bellies.
And most snakes only have a single
row of scales on their bellies.

LIZARD

Now, look closely at the picture on page 17.
Can you see why it is a lizard?

SNAKE

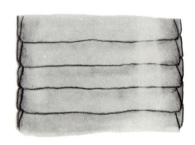

18

Is this another lizard without legs?

Look for ear openings.
There aren't any.

Look at its eyes. There are no eyelids.

Look at its belly. There is just
one single row of scales.

This must be a snake.

SNAKES

How can we tell snakes apart?
Most of them have pretty much the same shape.
But if you look closely you can find differences.

COPPERHEAD

WATERSNAKE

COACHWHIP

RUBBER BOA

Which snake has a head like its tail?

Which snake has a head shaped like a triangle?
(*Many poisonous snakes have this kind
of head. It is wise to stay away from all snakes
with triangular heads.*)

Which snake has a large, heavy body
and a short, narrow tail?

Which snake has a very long and
very thin body and tail?

Sometimes the skin pattern is a clue.

Look for the snake with rings around its body.
(*Stay away from all ringed snakes because
one kind, the coral snake, is very poisonous.*)

Look for the snake with only
one ring around its neck.

Look for the snake with stripes
running lengthwise.

RIBBON SNAKE

SCARLET KING SNAKE

RATTLESNAKE

Look for the snake with round spots
all over its body.

Look for the snake with diamond shapes
all over its body.
(*Notice the rattle at the end of its tail. All
snakes with rattles are poisonous. Stay away!*)
This snake also has a triangular head.

RINGNECKED SNAKE

ANACONDA

These three snakes are named after their noses.
Match the snake to its name.

HOOK-NOSED SNAKE   **LONG-NOSED TREE SNAKE**   **PATCH-NOSED SNAKE**

You can tell some snakes by the way they act
when they are disturbed.

Rattlers rattle their rattles.

Cobras spread their necks into hoods.

Racers whip through the grass with great speed.

Hog-nosed snakes spread their necks like
cobras. They may also roll over on their backs
and play dead.

TURTLES

Turtles are the only reptiles with shells.
Look at the shape of the shell.
Some turtles have shells that
are as flat as pancakes.

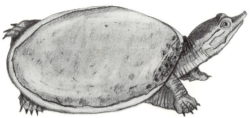

SOFTSHELL TURTLE

PAINTED TURTLE

Some turtles have shells that
are low and rounded.

Some turtles have shells that
are high and rounded.

BOX TURTLE

Some turtles have shells with a
high ridge down the back.
The ridge may have spines or knobs.

BLACK-KNOBBED SAWBACK

The shells of many turtles
are divided into flat, smooth plates.

FOREST TORTOISE

WOOD TURTLE

But sometimes the plates are bumpy.

And a few kinds of turtles have no plates at all.
This turtle has a smooth skin
with long ridges down the back.

LEATHERBACK TURTLE

27

There are other ways to tell turtles apart.

Find the turtle with a snout like a snorkel.

Find the turtle with legs like those of an elephant.

Find the turtle with a tail edged like a saw.
It also has a very long neck.

Find the turtle with feet shaped like paddles.

SNAPPING TURTLE

SOFTSHELL TURTLE

GREEN TURTLE

GIANT TORTOISE

28

Sometimes the pattern on the turtle's shell,
head, or legs gives it its name.

Match the turtle to its name.

DIAMONDBACK TURTLE   SPOTTED TURTLE   STAR TORTOISE

CROCODILES AND ALLIGATORS

The head of a crocodile is narrow and pointed.
It has one big tooth that shows
on each side of its mouth
even when its mouth is closed.

The head of an alligator is broad
and not pointed. No teeth show when its mouth
is closed.

Which is which?

When you look at a reptile—

Look at its shape.

Look at the pattern of its shell or skin.

Look at its scales or the plates on its shell.

Look for special parts.

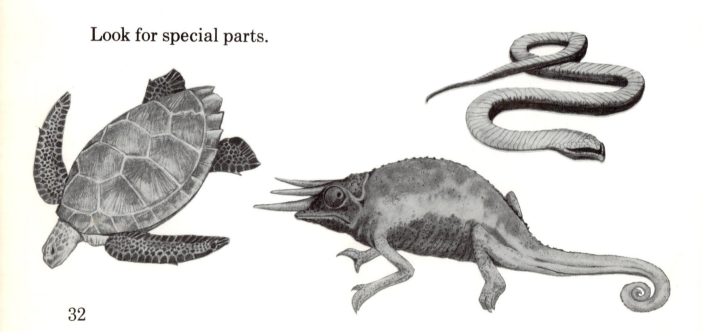

Date Due
